Kanban

*The Complete Step-by-Step Guide to Agile
Project Management with Kanban*

Jeffrey Ries

Table of Contents

Introduction

Congratulations on getting a copy of *Kanban: The Complete Step-by-Step Guide to Agile Project Management with Kanban* and thank you for doing so.

This book is your guide to learning the in's and out's of Kanban and how you can implement it successfully into your business. Kanban's simplicity is the major factor in how your teams can work together efficiently and produce effective projects in less time and for less money. You may have heard rumors that Kanban is "dead," but what you need to learn is how the world has evolved and implemented Kanban and other methodologies to improve their workplaces and workflows. Not all industries and organizations are suited to the Kanban system!

Are you a manufacturer looking to create a more lean process? Or are you developing software and want to deliver quality product faster? Or maybe you are a healthcare system struggling with inventory management? All of these scenarios are great situations for trying out Kanban. It is a simple, visual system that helps teams communicate effectively and take on only the work they can do within a desired time frame. When you are ready to roll it out to your team and stakeholders read over Chapter 6 to learn how Kanban improves workflow at your workplace so you can garner their buy in.

You are at the doorstep of learning not just what the core principles and practices of the Kanban system are, but how you can implement it well in your company. Read on to learn tips and techniques for creating digital boards, changing practices effectively, and gaining buy-in. Explore different approaches to a method with a long history of efficiency and productivity. If you are ready to save money, time and resources, then you are ready to implement Kanban.

There are plenty of books on this subject on the market, thanks again for choosing this one! Every effort was made to ensure it is full of as much useful information as possible, please enjoy!

Chapter 1

The Current Status of Kanban

The word "Kanban" is Japanese and its translation means "signal," "billboard," or "sign." The adaptation of the word "Kanban" describes a lean manufacturing process for delivering materials that need to be replenished by means of a signal, which is typically an empty space, empty bin, or a card. The system is designed for restocking materials when they are actually required; when a material has been completely consumed, thus creating a process founded on true need. Using this system correctly enables a company to minimize shortages, accomplish higher inventory turns, and tightly control their inventory.

Kanban development is rumored to be from processes employed in supermarkets in America in the mid-1900's. These stores would replenish products in smaller quantities based on their sales. In the 1950's, executives from Toyota came to visit the United States and took notice of the streamlined process in the supermarkets. Today, a lot of the Kanban process is attributed to Toyota's adaptation of this "supermarket" method.

In the 1990's, almost every business and industry was implementing Kanban lean methodology for delivering materials to their manufacturing line. For companies like Toyota, those that have a manufacturing system with an operator repeating their actions continuously, this was an ideal situation. For other industries, like machine shops or

Aerospace, this was more of a challenge. These organizations like Aerospace and machine shops ended up employing other material delivery systems, like a pick-list or kitting system. Pick-list is a list of materials needed for an order that the operator should gather for production. Kitting is when a manufacturer groups different but connected items into a bin to be assembled into a product.

It is important to remember that handling materials are wasteful, or as the Japanese say, "Muda." This is because handling materials do not add value to the end product. The touching of materials does not advance the final product's value. It is necessary to handle the materials for manufacturing a product, but you need to find the most efficient method to keep it minimal and productive. Throughput and efficacy are important for the people handling the materials and the operators on the manufacturing line that consume the materials.

There are five general situations when a Kanban method may not be the best for delivering materials:

1. The operator, or the person on the manufacturing line using the materials to make the product, has to turn around to reach the materials or even walk to get what they need to complete their job. These additional activities create even more waste in the process.
2. Sometimes two or more materials appear to be the same thing to the "naked eye" but they are different and mixing them up in the manufacturing process can cause a major error. If this is the case, like for similar-looking shims, a countermeasure is needed to prevent a mistake.
3. The rate for product completion is too short. This is called the *"takt"* time. When there is a limited amount of

time, a greater percentage of the time is required for part selection. This is true even if you have the products well distinguished and nearby.

4. Material usage is not consistent. When you offer a wide variety of products, but each product has a low volume, your bins will stay full. The unused materials are then taking up space and costing you money.

5. Materials must be traceable. Kanban does not allow you to mix loose materials into another bin for another lot. You need to keep a record of the lot used and document the materials not used. This is the best method for controlling a lot through a Kanban process, but it is more complicated than other, more loose processes.

If the traditional Kanban process is not right for all situations, what other choices are there? As mentioned earlier, Kitting and Pick-list are ideas. Kitting; however, is a "bad" word in the Lean community, so instead, think of it as a "Kanban Set." This methodology involves a selection of materials related to the sequence of building a specific product. An AGV or cart would bring the set to the manufacturing line. Because the set would not be delivered until is it signaled, usually by the return of an empty set or tray, it is considered a "pull" system.

A "pull" system means materials and products are delivered when an order is placed. This type of method is beneficial because it reduces the need for storing inventory. Lower inventory levels and reduced costs are the secondary benefits. The opposite of a "pull" system, is a "push" model. The "push" system is a forecast for inventory needs. The company then manufactures to meet the forecast and then pushes, or sells, it to their customers. The problem with this model is forecasts are typically wrong and results in many leftover products.

A product does not need to have just one "Kanban Set." To minimize material handling and movement, the materials could be chosen in smaller amounts. This process also minimizes the number of materials on the side of the line, which opens up more space on the production line. Materials coming in can have limited handling because the "Kanban Set" is placed in a logical location.

As an alternative to having materials on the line at each workstation, the "pick to light" process can be more efficient for the manufacturer. "Pick to light" is a system designed for fulfilling orders or manufacturing products. Normally the operator scans a barcode that is adhered to a tote or carton. These bins are a temporary holding place for materials. The scan reveals the location for materials so the operator can retrieve the necessary items. When the correct quantity of items is selected the operator presses a button to indicate the activity was completed. The operator continues to refill bins as indicated by this system until all materials are gathered for the manufacturing process.

What people have realized since the 1990's is that Kanban is still relevant, in the right situations. In other scenarios, like the ones mentioned earlier, quality, use of space, and labor inefficiency can result from trying to force a Kanban process where it does not belong. Instead, these situations should consider a "Kanban Set!"

Chapter 2

How to Utilize the Kanban Process in a Non-Manufacturing Setting

There are three primary parts to Kanban, no matter if you look at examples from a Toyota factory in the 1950s or on a Lean practitioners Kanban app. The three elements are board, list, and card. Essentially, the board contains a list, which creates the workflows from the various cards. Each is defined below:

1. Board- This is what houses the workflow. In other project management processes, this is referred to as a "workspace" or "project."

2. List- Also called a "lane," this has a series of aligned cards, usually related to the same part of the production line, and is the title of a column on a board. In other project management systems, it is called the "task list" or "to-do list."

3. Card- A card is found under a list title on a board. This is a product that needs to be created or a task that needs to be done. These are actionable items. In other systems, these are called "tasks" or "to-do's."

A Kanban board is as versatile as an Excel spreadsheet; its applications are endless. For example, if you are about to launch a new product, you can have two Kanban boards, one for marketing and one for development. Marketing would create a board with lists titled "Internal Promotion," "Press Pitches," and "Marketing Ideas." Development would create lists such as, "To-do," "Doing, and "Done." Each department would then create task cards to move from one column to the other as they bring up and complete each task.

While this example above only offers two ideas in a non-manufacturing setting, there are many more applications to explore. But no matter how you want to implement a board, you need to master the basics of moving from just having a list and a bunch of cards to developing an efficient and orderly workflow.

8 Primary Features of a Kanban Board

The features presented in this section all function primarily the same, no matter how you implement it. Some features only apply to an electronic version of the Kanban system, such as a Kanban app, while others apply to both a physical Kanban board and an electronic app. In addition, the names and titles may depend on the practitioner or app you use, but again, the functionalities are always similar.

1. Boards and Lists are Filled with Moving Cards

Being able to easily move cards around is critical to effectively utilizing Kanban boards. It is the most utilized feature in a Kanban model. In fact, the existing cards you have on the board will move more than the new ones you create. In an app, you can click on the card, hold down the button on your mouse, and move your cursor to a new location. This action allows you to move your card from one list to another or to change the location of the card on the existing list. Because this is a feature you will often utilize if you are using an app, find out what process works with the app you have chosen and become familiar with the layout and functionality as soon as possible. For example, LeanKit offers the ability to change list locations. You can have a higher or lower list, and you will need to know how to drag a card between them. Try it out and find where and how you can move your cards. After all, you cannot break it!

Unlike in a manual or physical board situation, you can look back the path each card has taken on your Kanban board. When you move a card on a physical board, you will either have to take pictures or mentally remember where it was to know its journey throughout the process. In an app, technology keeps track for you. In many apps, when you click on the card, it will "flip over" to reveal its backside. Here it will often show you its activity list. Much more efficient than the manual way!

2. People Are Invited To A Kanban Board, And Assignments Or Subscriptions Of Individual Cards Are Outlined.

As with other project management systems, collaborators, clients, and teammates can be invited to the project. An invitation can be extended through the app for access to the entire board or only for an individual card. Some apps only allow you to invite app members to the board while others will allow you to invite anyone by entering their name and email into the invitation fields. After they are added to the board, they can then act on the cards. If a member is added to a single card, they can only act on that card. Typically they can edit a card, comment on them, move or add them. In addition, they can also observe the stream of activity relevant to the board they are a part of. This allows the members to see the project process even if they are not an active part of the tasks.

To assign or share the responsibility of a task you can add a card to a member or user. This prompts the app to send notifications related to the activities for the card. If your card gets a comment, for example, you will receive a notification. If someone else is assigned that card, they will get the notification as well. When someone wants to follow the progress of a card but are not responsible for the activities, many apps provide the option to "subscribe" to it. This allows the member to monitor the activity and receive notifications but not act on the card. On the other hand, if you want to "unfollow" the activities of a card, you can unsubscribe from it. This is a good practice when you want to keep your inbox free from unnecessary notifications.

3. On the Backs of Cards, Include Notes or Communicate in Related Discussions

In a physical setting, your comments are confined to the size of a post-it. You can only communicate enough until the post-it is full. Then you run out of space, and the dialogue comes to a fork in the road. In a technological setting, space is boundless. This is another distinct advantage of a virtual board over a physical option. Now you can jot down everything necessary related to the card.

Typically, on the backside of the card, there are fields for card descriptions, a place to upload related files, and a discussion forum. Also, similar to tagging someone on Twitter, you can mention a person directly in the comment or description by writing, "@-(their username)." To access the back of the card, click on the card itself to flip it over or find the link that lists additional features for the card and select "back of card" or another similar phrase.

4. Cards Can Have Tasks or Checklists Attached

A card needs a checklist because each task is not always a simple situation. In a virtual board, the cards can contain 1 or more task lists or checklists to make the card more functional. Thinking back to the marketing example introduced at the beginning of this chapter, the marketing department had a list titled, "Press Pitches." Under this list, there is a card labeled, "Outreach." On this card there is a checklist containing the following to-do items:

- Create a preliminary email for the pitch
- Complete follow-up communication with additional details
- Deliver media assets
- Confirm coverage
- Publish coverage

In some apps, the front of the card illustrates the status and progress of the checklist, showing a stage of completion as each task is checked off. This way each member can easily see the progress of the card. Similar to discussions and notes, checklists can have specific member's names included by using the same format: "@-(their username)."

5. Limits to Work in Progress Included

For new practitioners, creating epic task lists can be exciting but overwhelming to all involved. This is why several apps provide the option to limit the number of tasks that can be created in a list and offer WIP's, or work in progress limits.

WIP's are pronounced like "whips." This restriction can be applied to one or all columns on a board, so you have a limit to the number of cards allowed on the list.

When you know the workload your team can realistically handle, you can set your limits accordingly. For example, if your marketing team can realistically produce 3 pitches per week, then set the limit for "Press Pitches" to no more than 3 cards.

6. Cards can be Tagged or Labeled

A "label" or "tag" allows you to clarify certain details of a card that cannot be immediately determined by its location on the list. Your administrator or app will determine if this clarification process is called "tagging" or "labeling." Both terms are synonymous at this point in the Kanban process.

For example, if a marketing idea is for an online publication and not for a print campaign, you can add a label to the card to denote that it will be published electronically. Maybe a card requires outside assistance from another department or one task is more challenging than another; both are situations where you need a clear label. Tags are created uniquely for each board you operate. Change the label's names and colors to fit the workflow for the board you are working on.

7. Due Dates can be Assigned to Cards

When there is not a due date on a card, it probably will not get done. Deadlines are essential to getting tasks completed.

Depending on the app you are using you can click on the clock icon on a card or find the field for the deadline on the back of the card. Typically there is a drop-down menu that allows you to select the date the card must be finished by.

Besides setting the date, the people assigned or subscribed to the card can also get notifications when the deadline is approaching and when something is considered overdue.

8. View a Calendar with Cards

Another added benefit of an electronic app is that it offers a seamless calendar view related to the board. In an app, the ability to switch from the "standard" board view to a calendar view is a simple toggle of a switch. This view will show all the advancing deadlines, schedules, and delivery dates for tasks. In this view you can also edit, move and add cards. If something is overdue or cannot be completed by its original deadline, you can drag the card to a new date to reset the deadline.

Trying Out Kanban

If you are interested in implementing the Kanban process in your business but want to test it out first, below are some ideas on how to start small before applying it to your whole company or department:

- Use a Kanban board for your personal to-do list
- Customize a calendar for editorial content
- Create a space to house ideas and content for projects
- Share a plan of action with teammates or clients
- Follow a sales funnel
- Develop a tracking system for applicants to streamline your hiring process

Chapter 3

Applying Kanban to Lean Manufacturing

Lean manufacturing and the Kanban process are often considered a natural pair. When a manufacturer wants to remove or reduce waste in their process, they use a methodical approach, which classifies them as "Lean." Because Kanban is a method for systematically replacing materials when needed, it is obvious why the two work well together.

The Function of Inventory Management in a Kanban Environment

There is a balance that the Kanban system looks to achieve between having the least amount of inventory possible and functioning at full capacity. This simple concept introduced by a supermarkets restocking process led to the introduction of Toyota's 6 principles of an efficient system:

1. The downstream remove materials in the exact amounts outlined by a Kanban system. "Downstream" can refer to customers, line operators, or anyone coming into contact with supplies or materials.

2. The upstream delivers materials in the exact amount and succession outlined by a Kanban system. "Upstream" can refer to the supplier, manager, or materials handler.

3. Movement or production does not happen without a Kanban task.

4. Every moment and every material should be part of a Kanban list or card.

5. The proceeding downstream should never receive incorrect or defective materials from their direct upstream.

6. The quantity of Kanban processes being used prudently lowers the levels of inventory while also improving the identification of problems in the current process.

In addition, the inventory actually being utilized is aligned with the need for that inventory. "Pulling" is often the term applied to this concept. A signal is sent when a certain material is exhausted. This signal tells the supplier it is time to send more products and consequently an order is tracked in the cycle for replenishment. This simple method also tracks the frequency of necessary restocking. Cards or bins are used to signal the need for refilling specific products.

In Lean manufacturing, bins are a popular method for tracking. A bin process provides a visual indication to start the process of restocking. An operator or employee is given two bins to work from. They are to pull materials from the first bin until it is exhausted, and then they move to the second bin. When the employee moves to the second bin, the first empty bin sends a signal to the line manager to reorder materials. In an efficient system, the employee will be replenished with materials before the second bin is depleted. To decide how many materials should be placed in a bin, first determine how long it will take the supplier to deliver materials and then how long it takes for your operator to deplete one bin.

Pros and Cons of Kanban in Lean Manufacturing

For lean manufacturing, using a logical process for inventory monitoring and customer demand fulfillment makes rational business sense. That is why the Kanban system makes so much sense for this type of application. Despite it being a sound pairing, some considerations must be addressed before a concrete process can be implemented. Recognizing the several pros and possible cons for Kanban lean manufacturing allows your business to implement a Kanban process effectively.

Pros of using a Kanban Inventory Management Process in Lean Manufacturing

1. **Lowers the costs and levels of inventory**. Workspace is increased when there is less inventory cluttering the area. Also, providing the minimum

quantity of inventory saves money. The business does not purchase materials that will not be used.

2. **Need is determined by the demands of the customer**. When materials and products are exhausted, you can identify best-selling products. If a product hardly ever needs new parts restocked, you can assume it has a low demand by your customer.

3. **Production is to deliver, not to store**. The line only gets the materials necessary to deliver what is needed. The saved storage space now opens more room on the line for assembly. Also, fewer mistakes are made in grabbing incorrect products because they are being stored on the floor and not a storeroom.

4. **Progress reports reach managers organically**. If your company is using Kanban software or apps to monitor the process, many provide analytics to illustrate the volume of products being constructed and the time frame required for completion. A more integrated Kanban software system can provide a variety of reports to help with improving, organizing, and planning the workflow accordingly.

5. **Decreases archaic inventory**. Excess inventory causes a lot of extra work and consideration for a manufacturer. In addition to finding storage space for it, the company must determine how long to hold on to it, and what to do when it comes time to get rid of it. For example, the manufacturer can decide to throw it away or give it away or try to sell it themselves. Also, when there is stagnant inventory, damaged inventory is more likely to continue downstream. Finding a

problem during shipping is the worst-case scenario, especially if it has been taking up time and space for several months. Once it hits the floor the options for dealing with it are limited. It is best to decrease inventory that is not being immediately handled.

6. **Overproduction rarely occurs.** Pulling only happens when materials are needed. Necessity is determined by the demands of the customer. This process means that all the products are selling, and no excess is created.

Cons of using Kanban's Inventory Manufacturing Process in Lean Manufacturing

Before jumping head first into a Kanban inventory management system, you need to do a few things that take time and consideration. First, you must observe the number of materials already being used. This will tell you the amount of stock needed for reordering. This observation can take a large amount of time, depending on your products. This means bins and material levels in the bins will fluctuate as you respond to the patterns and needs. This observational period can slow down production. Production can also be delayed if you do not factor delivery time properly for restocking bins. Consider a bin filled with seven materials. The line takes about 14 days to deplete the bin. This means the supplier will need to deliver more stock between 10 to 12 days. Otherwise, your production will lag. It is common to have these types of delays or fluctuations during the initial observation and implementation period.

How to Create a 2-bin Inventory Management System

After you have established a firm grasp on your inventory flow and reordering methods, you will need to implement your 2-bin inventory system. It will take a bit of time to work out the "kinks," but after a while, you will get it to work seamlessly. Below is a mathematical system developed by Oracle that can assist you:

$D * A * (L + SSD) = (C - 1) * S = $ *Amount of Materials per Bin*

D = Avg. demand for a particular product each day
A = Apportionment currently
L = Replenishment time required for inventory
SSD = "Safety Stock Days"
C = Quantity of cards
S = Size of board

"Safety Stock Days" refers to a "buffer" of time added between when a delivery should arrive and when it is needed on the floor. This is used in case an emergency arises or there is a problem with the shipment.

Software for Inventory Management

Over the past few years tracking inventory and materials have become easier than ever thanks to the introduction of things like software, RFID, and barcodes. Software has been developed to provide automated solutions to a Kanban process. Using a combination of the two-bin visual system with an integrated Kanban software system, your production line, and inventory management has the opportunity to become efficient and profitable. Integrating and automating a Kanban process helps direct your entire supply chain. Besides watching for the signal and restocking materials when needed, the system can track lead times and replenishment times. It can also alert you if a material will be replenished in time for the line or if it is going to cause a delay. The system provides reports about how well the line is producing and what products are selling. Even in a lean manufacturing setting the Kanban production process crosses several departments, so it is important to manage it properly and allow stockholders to view the process.

Chapter 4

Applying a Kanban Process to Software Development

Software development has been using various project management philosophies for decades now, but that raises the question why you would choose a Kanban system over other methodologies, such as SCRUM, or resources, similar to a Gantt chart? To begin, you need to review the differences between the main methodologies.

Kanban vs. Other Methodologies

SCRUM is still a popular project management process used in software development today. While it is another successful, agile project management approach, there is a major difference between the Kanban process and SCRUM.

For example:

- A Kanban system does not include time boxes like SCRUM requires.
- A Kanban system has fewer tasks, and they are larger than SCRUM tasks.
- A Kanban system does not assess the process often, if at all, as it does in a SCRUM environment.

- A Kanban system only considers the average completion time for a project instead of basing project time on the "speed of the team," like in a SCRUM setting.

For practitioners who are used to the SCRUM environment, thinking that a project is made up of the team's speed, increased dimension, and scrum meetings, may find the idea of removing them outrageous. Those activities are the primary methods for controlling development in a SCRUM system! The real problem with this concept is the illusion of control. Managers are constantly striving for this control, but the reality is that they will never obtain it. A manager's supervision and influence only work if the team wants to work. If they collectively decide not to push for a project's completion, it does not matter what the manager does; the object will fail.

Imagine a different scenario: one where people have fun at work and work efficiently. Managers then need not control the environment. Control in this setting would actually disrupt the situation and raise the cost. In a SCRUM setting, controlling measures add costs by requiring constant discussions, meetings, and time commitments during the changing of sprints. Most sprints require one day to wrap up and one day to start the next. Those extra days could be considered "wasted" opportunity. If you look at it as a percentage, a 2-week sprint requires 20% of the time to be spent in preparing and wrapping up. That is a lot of time! In some SCRUM environments, as much as 40% of the time can be spent on supporting the methodology and not on completing the mission.

The Kanban system; however, focuses on tasks. This differs greatly from a SCRUM process. SCRUM practitioners want a successful sprint. Kanban practitioners want completed tasks. Tasks in a Kanban system are approached from start to finish, not bound to a sprint time frame. The completed work is presented, and the project is deployed based on when it is ready. Tasks do not have an estimated time for completion set by the team. The reason is that there is no need for this time estimate, and an estimate is often wrong, anyway. If a manager believes and supports their team why would an estimate be necessary? Would not the team want to produce the best they can in the fastest time possible? The manager instead focuses their own attention on developing a pool of prioritized tasks. The team's focus is on completing as many tasks as possible from the pool. It is that simple. Control measures are unnecessary. Managers add items to the pool and reorganize the priorities of tasks as needed. That is how a Kanban practitioner runs a software project.

Sample Kanban Lists for Software Development

Sample lists or columns on a Kanban board for software development include:

1. *GOALS.* Useful but optional. Major goals can be placed here. This is more for a regular reminder to the team than it is an actionable list.

2. *STORY.* On-deck tasks are placed on this list. The card on the top is the highest priority. The team then takes the top card and moves it to the next column, typically labeled "develop."

3. *ELABORATE AND ACCEPT.* Other descriptions can be used for this column before they proceed to the "done" list. Each team and workflow differs from one another. Anything that is uncertain for the team's approach, like an approach to a code that is unfinished or designs that are not determined, can be assigned to this list. The team then needs to discuss and decide on how to handle it before moving it to the next list.

4. *DEVELOP.* Until the task is complete, the card stays on the "develop" list. It does not matter what needs to be completed for the card or task, but if there is anything that needs to be done before the task is complete, it is placed on this list.

5. *DONE.* Once a card is on this list, it indicates that the task has been completed. It signals to the team that nothing further is needed for this task.

This suggested layout means that any list or column can contain a high-priority task. Each task on the board should be completed as soon as possible. Sometimes there is a column made for only high-priority items. This could be in the "goals" column, or another column labeled "expedite." This signals the team that all items on the list need to be completed first. This means anything placed on this list are of the highest importance only. All other items should be placed on the "story" list until "expedite" items are finished.

Other interesting features on a Kanban board are the numbers located under each list or column. These numbers determine the number of cards, or tasks, that are permitted to each list. This is also called "work in progress" or "WIP's." These numbers are not scientifically determined but are rather chosen by the manager according to their discretion. Typically the number is related to the number of developers assigned to the list. It represents the capacity of the team for work. For example, if there are eight developers, "develop" may be given a number four. Putting two will result in bored team members, and they will talk to each other too much. Putting eight will result in each person working on their task but staying on the list too long. This means the focus on the Kanban process is forgotten; the length of time spent on a task to be completed from the start until the finish is not shortened.

The Benefits of a Kanban System to the Software Development Team

There are several reasons a Kanban process is beneficial to your software development team. To start, several tasks can be completed at one time, cutting back on the time required for completing each of them. The actions taken are only the necessary ones, so there is no switching frameworks or tracking various articles. Planning is unnecessary. Tasks are developed when the project begins, not before. Next, "showstoppers" or problems in the process are identified and solutions are found together as a team to keep the process moving forward.

For example, if a task requires the assistance from another department, but the other department is working on another series of tasks, the production of the project must halt. But an efficient Kanban team recognizes the need for teamwork and will band together to solve the problems so all departments can continue to function efficiently. Finally, it is possible to calculate the completion time of average tasks. Cards can be tracked according to their initiation date, all movements on the board, and when it was completed. Even wait times between each step can be averaged. This information can be valuable to a manager's calculations for planning purposes.

The Rules of Kanban

There are only 3 primary requirements in a Kanban setting, even for software development:

1. Production is visual:

   a. Tasks or cards are created to divide work. The cards are then added to the board.
   b. The board contains lists presented as individual columns. Cards are located in a column in order of priority.

2. Each part of production works to minimize WIP, or "work in progress," which refers to the maximum amount of work being completed concurrently.

3. Shortening the amount of time spent on the process is the purpose of consistently working to develop the system and determine the average time for a task to be completed. This time is determined by measuring the time for each step in the production cycle.

These are the only three requirements of a Kanban system! SCRUM contains nine primary requirements. XP requires 13. The traditional RUP process has over 120! This alone illustrates the major difference and benefit of Kanban in software development.

Chapter 5

How Kanban Reduces Risk and Creates Improved Software

It is amazing that a pull system created by a supermarket and adapted to a car manufacturing company can help software development companies create quality products with reduced risk, but it works. The largest difference is that instead of pulling physical materials from bins, the Kanban agile project management system improves organizational throughput in a software environment. Tasks are "pulled" into the work pipeline when it is required. Schedules and forecasts are not what "pushes" it into production.

Throughput is improved in a software system by:

- Reducing WIP, or work in progress
- Every development phase is unassumingly observed
- Predictability of an organization is improved through metrics and reports
- Minimal impact results from steps towards change that are incremental, evolutionary, small, and continuous
- Capacity to self-manage is developed by motivating and increasing opportunity for the teams
- The actual management of tasks and knowledge of work processes is promoted through the team
- The risks and issues facing the team are discussed objectively and rationally

Software teams accomplish these actions by following a Kanban process.

Work is Visual

The board is the tool used to show the various stages of work at a micro-level. Using this tool highlights the problems and roadblocks before they become a devastating "fire." At a very basic level, the board contains three lists or columns. They are "to do," "doing," and "done." By showing them in columns, the team can easily identify what is left in each phase. This process simply shows the progress of a project without having to update a stakeholder manually by other means like a call or email.

Visualizing the work assists the organizational throughput by:

- Breaking down individual steps from "A" to "Z"
- Every step includes a column, or list, to facilitate a smoother pipeline execution and delineation
- Easier at-a-glance monitoring is thanks to the color-coding assigned to various types of work if used
- Work status is available in a central location to inform relevant people of the progress of the project

Cards can be moved from column to column easily, updating team members in real-time so they can swiftly act on any problems or challenges early on.

WIP is Limited

Using up your time multitasking is something to be avoided in an agile environment. Taking on several tasks at one time opens the developer up to making more errors, each deliverable takes more time, and the cycle for delivery takes longer. The limits placed on the WIP means nothing can be added until something is removed and the limit is chosen in relation to the capabilities and capacity of the team. When each phase is able to take on more work, it is pulled from another place, not pushed on top of existing expectations.

Projects are divided into smaller pieces, and each is tackled independently in a Kanban process. This makes workflow steady and swift. Limits clog the pipeline, but for a valid reason. When something clogs the system, the team is in charge of "cleaning" the clog before adding in new work to the pipeline.

WIP limits assist organizational throughputs by:

- Maintaining time management through an effective structure and system. No matter the size of the team or how complex or simple the project is there is an unvarying process for each task to be finished in a limited timeframe.
- A smooth workflow removes waste from your schedule, resources, and cost. In addition, it eliminates work that is unnecessary. This is the primary function of limits for WIP.

Changes are Incremental

Changes that are completed incrementally develop your current actions in an effort to continually move the project forward. Identifying the joints in the system that cause work to back up is another benefit of a Kanban system. WIP limits are engaged in an early stage to complete work fast and inject new work in a controlled manner. As work moves to each new stage, the limits placed on WIP are refined and the phases change, the improvements to the workflow are more obvious. "Evolutionary" is the term applied to the Kanban methodology because the approach to the work is completed in bite-sized increments.

Incremental changes improve throughput by:

- Constant improvement accomplished at each stage of the process. All the way until the final, "done" step the results are quality deliverables and final outputs are less prone to errors.

Flow Enhancement

In a traditional environment, sometimes the developers can lack the understanding of what to do following the completion of the task they were assigned. This confusion probably occurs because the earlier work had a bug found in it. If this occurs, the developers do not understand what their next course of action should be because the work is considered finished and they have already pulled new work up and updated the board. Implementing a Kanban system prevents this from happening because the next work task that is pulled onto the board and placed in a list is the highest priority task in the backlog.

Following this process lessens crisis and confusion that frequently occurs when there is an unavailable resource. "Done" work can only occur when the product is finalized and in use. This process saves time and reduces the quantity of re-work necessary.

Organizations that adopt a Kanban system find that the time and effort put into the adoption phase is worth it. The challenges of trying a new agile system like this reap several benefits, including reducing risk and improving the outcome. Employing the mechanisms outlined above in this chapter illustrates the way Kanban assists software development teams, which sometimes these teams can be scattered across the globe, onto the same page. This is feasible thanks to virtual boards and integrated Kanban software. These systems provide easily viewable WIP and strategy to provide tracking systems for project status and individual tasks. These tools are designed to make a Kanban system easier for your team.

Developmental processes are also benefited through the implementation of a Kanban system. Bottlenecks are identified, and workflow is efficiently tracked through this methodology. This means if you are searching for an improved throughput for your software development, a Kanban process provides a powerful solution to your needs. Now you can offer exceptional software to your clients in the best delivery time possible while simultaneously lowering the risks associated with the process.

Chapter 6

Applying A Kanban Process to Workflow in Your Company

While a Kanban process can be applied to manufacturing and software development, many organizations do not engage in physical products. Consequently, industry leaders have taken notice of the Kanban system and discovered application methods for it in knowledge or creative environments. Jim Benson and David J. Anderson led the charge to adopt the Kanban process improvements in their business. These changes were embraced by others and have been used by companies for decades, enjoying similar efficiency and quality.

For example, a marketing department can re-imagine their creative process as a "production" line with requests for features beginning at one point and improving the results coming off the line at the other side. Like in other industries, showing a visual process of work from start to finish allows a business to improve their workflow. It shows bottlenecks early in the process and encourages all the WIP to be finished in the time anticipated.

Knowledge work, like your company's workflow, can follow the four steps of the Kanban process effectively.

Workflow Can Be Visual

Just like in a manufacturing or software development environment, the work and workflow are visualized in a Kanban system. This process allows team members and stakeholders the ability to see the process of work tasks. Results and communication are then improved thanks to the transparency of the process, including all the lines of work, bottlenecks, and "showstoppers." Some teams prefer to have a whiteboard with post-it's while others prefer a digital system for displaying the board. Whatever method your company adopts, the purpose is to show how work is moved from start to finish, no matter how "good" or "bad" it appears.

Work in Progress is Limited

The demand is what pulls a task to another stage. Demand can be from the customer, or it can be from an opening in the downstream. Whatever the case, it is similar to a "just in time" objective. Given a specific time frame, the limit for what is manageable for your team is set for your pipeline's capacity. To illustrate, consider a design team. They are not limited to producing a set amount of deliverables related to what the marketing team can use in a campaign.

Flow is the Focus

The beginning of the end of the project is free to flow when there is a limit placed on the work in progress, and it is a visual workflow. The formation of backlogs can be prevented by the early identification and resolution of the bottlenecks. These interruptions can be resolved before they cause a major breakdown in production. This is true in a creative workplace, just as it is in manufacturing. For example, if the design team has trouble taking on a certain amount of graphic design before heading to web marketing, then it is easy to identify a need for additional resources, training, or alternative limitations. This early identification is critical to three factors: conflicts are prioritized based on the "showstopper," the value to the customer remains high and they stay close to the project, and the investment continues to have a positive return for the company. If the work lags in the process, the investment is tied up, the customer's value decreases, and conflicts are mismanaged.

On a Kanban board, there is a number assigned to each group, column, or list. This number identifies the workload the team can realistically produce in a week or another given time frame. When a list is at capacity, it is considered "blocked." This means that nothing can be added to the list until something moves and creates space for it. A task that is moved must go to another list, including the "done" list. If a manager recognizes that a list is constantly "blocked," they can address the backlog before things pile up beyond functionality. For example, if work is completed, but it is waiting for QA to open up to review the work, and items continue to sit and wait for QA, a manager can see the jam and work to address the issue to get the project moving again.

Improvement is Constantly Happening

Improvement opportunities are identified thanks to the continuous analysis and monitoring that the Kanban methodology requires. Quality, the pace of production, the flow tracked throughout the process is what is used to measure the effectiveness of the team. Being able to visualize the workflow for the company is an immensely valuable instrument used by any business to improve the procedures of their workplace. For the "overachiever," who often takes on more work than they can handle, benefits from the limitations placed on the work in progress. A daily and weekly restriction of tasks makes sure your team members do not try to multitask, ultimately costing you time and money. Instead, they are free to produce quality work in the shortest time possible.

A Kanban process is a simple, agile approach, but its efficiency and effectiveness are hard to rival. It assists teams in operating at a higher productivity level, minimizes conflict, and provides an even distribution of value to your clients. If your organization values improvement on a continuous basis, a Kanban system is a reduced-risk and reduced-cost option to consider.

How Kanban Can Fit Any Workplace Team and Workflow

Maybe you are running an organization with several project management teams, or maybe you are a small company with only a couple people dedicated to an agile project. It does not matter the size of your company; a Kanban system can fit in with your organizational goals. Ultimately, implementing this agile project management methodology will offer you peace and prosperity in your company (and often your own life!).

Tell a Complex Story Through a Simple Board

The first thing you see when you enter a company implementing a Kanban process is a gorgeous board. Maybe this board is a colorful array of post-its scattered across various columns, or it is a sleek online board with interactive cards and lists. No matter the version you see, it is there, and it is beautiful. The aesthetic appeal alone makes it a great tool to select to manage your organization and strategize workflow. Consider the phrase, "a picture is worth a thousand words." Yet a Kanban board is worth more than that! A scan of the board reveals the movement of tasks in the project. Things like completed tasks, the state of each task, and the progress of each task are evident, along with even more information. There will be no struggle to find more information about a project. It is all at your fingertips and visual plane with the Kanban board.

Simplicity Means No Learning Curve

Using a board is a simple process. It does not require extensive training to learn how to operate one. The stages of your project are divided easily, and the board is "decorated" with your tasks in specific categories. Each task is assigned to a team member. When the team member assigned to it completes a task, they are able to place it into the next, downstream list. This whole process is self-explanatory, meaning you can save time by not training your team on how to use it. Once you decide to adopt a Kanban system, it is possible to be up and running as a Kanban organization in just a few days.

Shifting Priorities can be Accounted for Quickly

When a customer specifies what they want at the beginning previous project management systems made the assumption that these requirements are frozen until delivery. In reality, this is not what happens. Priorities constantly change over and over again. When the scope changes, a manager needs to shift priorities with it. Changes are easily managed on a Kanban board. Even small changes can be made quickly and visually on the board. When you are using an electronic board, then even the team members assigned to the changed task are alerted.

Your Workplace Runs with Your Workflow

As you create a visual Kanban organization, your work will begin to run more smoothly alongside your workflow. You will see everything, address issues early, and keep the process moving. The hard work is alleviated with the simplicity of Kanban boards. It is flexible, visual, flowing, and easy.

Chapter 7

Implement A Kanban System Effectively

Your organization can understand lean management easily because it is such a simple method for improving business activity. To illustrate the simplicity of a lean methodology, you cannot get a better example than the Kanban process. It is a tool that controls the flow of information and materials. Despite its simplicity, many organizations are still confused by the concept. Maybe it is because it is so simple. Implementing Kanban should be easy, but it is often implemented below its true potential. This then leads to the process being abandoned. This is why implementing it effectively is so critical.

Below are rules, guidelines, and considerations necessary to a successful Kanban system implementation. Before you begin the process of implementation, consider the following:

A Kanban process can be:

- A device to communicate from the operation last conducted to the usage point. Or, from the supplier to the customer.
- P.O.'s provided to your suppliers.
- Orders for work to your areas of manufacture.
- A tool for visual communication.
- A method for reducing paperwork.

A Kanban system should not be used for:

- Batch or lot or single item production. Something you only create a few times a year should not be managed with a Kanban process.
- Stock designed or used for safety purposes.
- Inventory held by a supplier. For example, consignment or dropshipping is not appropriate for a Kanban system. This situation is not considered a "win-win" lean situation.
- A tool to plan long-term. Traditional management methodologies are best for situations like introducing new products, changes to a customer's usage, and changes in engineering.

To start, within your company, select one area to implement a Kanban system. Begin implementation with less than eight items in this area. Alert your business regarding the implementation and answer questions they raise about how the methodology works. Once the initial implementation is successful and smooth in the one area of your organization, consider adding more areas or items to the process.

Guidelines for Successful Implementation

1. Prior to implementing a Kanban process:

    - A reduction is arranged. If this is ignored than the typical process, a "batch production," continues because the sizes of orders are still large.
    - Production and requirements are uniform or level. Kanban can work for complex situations, but when it is early in the implementation phase, it is best, to begin with, requirements that are more uniform.

2. Suppliers outside your organization need to be certified. The history of the supplier's outside quality is the reasons for not requiring the inspection of their deliveries. This way "on hold" or "rejected" deliveries do not prevent the workflow.

3. Choose a bright color for any Kanban related container, cart, or tote and paint them all. A vibrant green is a good choice if you are stuck on what to choose. This allows all members of your organization to recognize a Kanban tool, especially during the implementation phase. It is also an easy way to keep track of all the materials necessary for your new system, ensuring all items stay in their correct place.

4. "Supermarkets" are a good tool to use if you use it well:

    - A "supermarket" provides a temporary place for a supplier to house items that are between the customer and the user.

49

- This is best employed when several customers are internal and rely on a supplier that is external. Another reason to employ a "supermarket" is when several customers are internal, and a supplier is also internal.
- This method provides a barrier between the many customers and the supplier, so the supplier does not receive several signals from all the requests.
- The "supermarket" sends the only signal to the supplier that is at the highest priority

The Rules For Implementing a Kanban Process in Your Organization

1. Your customers, suppliers, stakeholders, and entire organization need to be involved in your implementation. Do not even try to launch a Kanban process without their knowledge. Anyone that adds value to the chain of production needs to be included. After all, these are the people that support and report your company as a revolutionary. They must be a part of the revolution, too.

2. The source is the origination point for quality. Customers should never receive a defective product or poor information. Immediate correction is required. Otherwise, you risk losing your customer's pipeline.

3. Support equipment must be reliable. Choose an area to implement a Kanban system where there is TPM or Total Productive Maintenance.

4. Lead times and setup should be short. Requirements for delivery should occur evenly every month. This means a Kanban system should be focused on parts and products that are consistent. Reduce setup and efforts to minimize the lead-time for raw materials for items that differ each month according to the requirements of the customer.

5. Programs to reduce setup at the supplier level, whether external or internal, should be developed. If they do not have their own program in place, you should assist them with one. Lead times and the capacity to manufacture should not be influenced by the time required to set up. That is the only time when a Kanban process should be implemented.

6. Customers should receive the supplier's materials directly. Non-certified suppliers, or those that still require inspection upon delivery, require the usage point to do the inspection. If this is not possible, then a certified supplier should replace the option in use.

7. Trial and error are necessary to find how it will work best for your company. This is because nothing is fixed. When there are changes to the level of sales or containers or cards are reduced because activities are continuously improved, you need to be ready to make changes to your system. This is especially important during the implementation stage of the Kanban system.

How to Implement a Kanban Process Effectively

Once you identify the area and actions you want to address with a Kanban process to begin, you will want to follow the steps outlined below:

1. Create a visual of what you want to accomplish. Assemble a series of photographs that show off how it should look along with a label that is clear and definitive. Make it so simple that even someone not working in your organization can understand it.

2. Theorize the consumption of the product on a daily basis. Use your own observations, data, or ask your employees about how much consumption possibly occurs. Accuracy is not essential at this point. Keep this step simple.

3. Determine how or what you will use to send a signal. Consider things like cards, containers, spaces, color, and if you will use a digital or manual system. If you are completely new to using a Kanban system, consider keeping it simple and doing it by hand to try it out. Do not get caught up in the fancy, expensive software system unless you are ready to expand your Kanban process to other areas or more items.

If the materials are heavy, do not use bins. Instead, use carts that roll. Choose a bright color, like a vibrant green as suggested in the previous chapter. If your colors are vibrant green, choose something different. This process requires you to make choices based on your common sense. Decide what you think is best and try it out. You can always alter your choice if you find it is not the best fit.

4. The quantity of Kanban cards or bins must be calculated. This is done through a mathematical equation:

Kanban # = Daily Qty X Lead Time in Days X (1 + ss) / Qty Inside the Container

- Kanban # - The number of cards or containers
- Daily Qty – The number of pieces utilized each day on average
- Lead Time in Days – Estimate how many days a depleted material is replenished. Always estimate more days than you think necessary to be safe.
- (1 + ss) – Stock for safety is "ss." Typically this is either 10% or 15%. In the equation, ss will appear as 0.1 or 0.15.
- Qty Inside the Container – Choose a number that will provide you with between 1 to 5 days of consumption. Sometimes the number in a box from the supplier will make sense to your production line while other times it will not. Use common sense to set an original estimate and adjust as you implement the process.

To provide you with an example situation, imagine the following:
- *Kanban # - Unknown*
- *Daily Qty – 60*
- *Lead Time in Days – 5*
- *(1 + ss) – 10%*
- *Qty Inside the Container – 15 items*

The equation will appear as such:

Kanban # = 60 X 5 X (1 + 0.1) / 15

The answer then reveals:

Kanban # = 22

This is the number of cards or carts you will use in your Kanban.

5. Assign roles to team members. Make sure each role understands what is expected of them. For example, a user must understand and agree to your estimations. They must also place the signal in the designated location and participate in the process. There is also a role for the person responsible for moving signals, cards, and restarting the process. The people in the warehouse also play a critical role that you assign. They are the ones refilling containers or carts with the appropriate materials.

This means that they need to know what to do when they get the signal. Finally, you need to assign the facilitator role to the Kanban process. You typically fill this role; however, you can hire an outside contractor or professional to fill this role or assign someone from your team. This role is present during the entire process and can assist in training and problem solving with the rest of the team. To successfully implement Kanban to your project, this role must be filled with an active participant for a minimum of 1 month.

Basically, engaging your people and providing the tools of the Kanban system is the best way to implement a Kanban process successfully. It can resolve production problems or illustrate deficiencies in your line. It can save you time and money. But if you do not roll it out well, you can end up making stakeholders and clients unhappy, disgruntled your employees, slow production time, and cost your company money. This is why, despite the simplicity of the Kanban methodology, it is important that you take your time and launch it well. Having employees and stakeholders focused on the goal, while your line is producing quality work steadily at a fast pace, and waste is reduced is all worth it!

Chapter 8

Implement Kanban Digital Boards for Production

So you have decided to implement a Kanban process. Maybe it is because you are not meeting deadlines. Or maybe it is because your company has grown and your original organizational strategy no longer fits. Whatever the reason, implementing Kanban boards to help with your production is a valid solution.

As introduced in an earlier chapter, there are a couple versions of a Kanban process you can introduce: manual or electronic. While there are great advantages to having a manual board, with post-its and dry erase markers, there is something extra special to using a digital board. Consider all the planning necessary to set up a Kanban board. You need to consider your project to alleviate your tasks each day. The concept again is simple, but the application, meaning the setup of your digital board, must be done correctly. Yes, there is a "wrong" way.

A basic Kanban board has three lists, presented as columns, titled "to do, "doing," and "done." The cards are listed in a relevant column, the highest priority placed on the top of the list or assigned a specific color. This is your starting point. Maybe you operate a company that succeeds with this basic method, but maybe you need more. No matter your needs, the first thing you need to do is always the same: plan.

The Planning Phase

Setting up a board and haphazardly creating cards in random columns is not an effective strategy for using your board. The planning phase occurs before anything is added to your board. This phase can be challenging or easy, depending on your industry and company design. For example, manufacturing finds the planning phase to be easy because their process is more static, while knowledge and creative industries have a more complex planning process because the needs and items change frequently. Manufacturing creates lists for each process step and assigns a task to a person or team. For knowledge industries, it is necessary to consider the work to be completed and how they view the tasks required to complete the workflow.

Before setting up your board, you need to plan your workflow and create your digital board. In knowledge-based industries, digital is clearly the best because it can include comments, a visual platform for all interested parties no matter their geographic location, and an easy method for adding or editing tasks.

Below are the steps involved in the planning process:

1. Reality should be used to create a map for your procedures. Model it as closely as possible. Goals that are unrealistic are counterproductive to your purpose. The job considering needs to be assigned to a trained and skilled team member. Especially in the beginning, allow your team to have a more malleable time frame. You can adjust this as you observe the process as it improves.

2. Improvement in your workflow is the goal of the metrics designed for your board. Make sure what you add includes the correct metrics to accomplish this. The completion of the project will see several changes, therefore, allow for changes to occur on the board. Nothing is solidified on your board, at least not yet. This is still a planning phase, so everything is still a "work in progress."

3. Problems that often occur, like concealed work or lag time, now need to be considered. Projects often go over on time or turn a new direction because problems constantly arise. This is an important consideration. When you encounter a problem like an "on hold" task because there is a lag time from the supplier or a team member is working on another task, jot down the information. On the next project, identify the challenge concisely and clearly to help the team overcome the issue for the future.

Simplicity on Your Board is Important

A digital board serves one simple, primary purpose: make your life easier. Overcomplicating the content on the board is, therefore, an indirect contradiction to its purpose. Since the idea of the board and the Kanban methodology, in general, is simple, people will get on board fast, but if you keep adding content and changing tasks, they may have a hard time keeping up. Placing a lot of information on the board at one time can also overwhelm your team. It can be especially overpowering if it is new to the team. In addition, you do not want to surprise the team with tasks that were not discussed with them or columns that are unnecessary. Before adding anything new to the list, talk it over with the team, and do not have more than four columns on the board at one time.

Over-simplicity on your Board is Dangerous

If over complication is to be avoided, so is over-simplification. Creating a bare board means your team is less likely to show interest in it. They will not need to refer to it every day, and will then most likely forget about it. The board should provide a method for communication and teamwork on a daily basis. This means you need to organize it well and update it often. This will make sure there is always something new for your team to interact with.

How to Set Up Your Digital Board

Follow the steps below to successfully set up your digital Kanban board:

1. Determine your Kanban software system for your digital board.

2. Begin with the basic setup of your board with three lists titled "to do," "doing," and "done."

3. Limit your team's WIP to prevent overwhelming them. Too many tasks occurring simultaneously can be crushing.

4. Empower your team to choose the items they will work on based on their abilities. This is the foundation of a pull system and a benefit of many of the agile methodologies, including a Kanban methodology.

5. Organize the planning and prioritizing steps. Using demand to prioritize and select items is ensured when you set this up properly.

After the initial set up of your digital board, observe the needs of your organization and adjust accordingly. Consider also looking online, for example, Kanban boards for your industry to help get ideas on how to best structure your own. Finding examples and adjusting the settings to fit the needs of your team by empowering them to produce efficiently is the plan after the initial set up.

"Good" versus "Bad" Boards

The setup of your board can be deemed "good" or "bad" for a variety of reasons, but no matter how it is classified, you need to understand the difference between the two. What works for one company may not be the best for another. A team can remain focused on the project vision with a process that is parallel for all the developers in a small environment. "To do" and "done" are shared amongst the team, but the "doing" lane is filled with horizontal lines. This layout allows the small team to show what steps they are individually completing in association with the entire team's project. Structuring the board this way is great because board changes are easily made, avoiding having to mess with the "to do" and "done" sections. All the team members involved will appreciate the simple flow.

But what if you have a large team? Trying to keep all the tasks for a large group on one board will result in an overly complicated system. All the tasks that people are working on will make the overall flow seem confusing, thus negating the reason for using a Kanban method. Thin out your process that is placed on the board and make it easy for them to use the tool. This could mean creating different boards for sub-groups or sub-teams or creating a list just for a particular action or group. Again, you need to find a solution that works for your team environment and process.

Chapter 9

Development Tips for Your Kanban Digital Boards

Below are the top tips for maximizing your digital Kanban board. Refer to this chapter often as you begin and continue your Kanban implementation to make sure you are "checking off" the items on the "good" list and are getting the most out of your efforts.

The "Good" List

To determine if your list is "good," see if you can check off all the items on the list below. If you are missing an item, revisit your planning process to correct your board for your team. You want your digital board to check off all the items here:

- Chose to use a **digital format or a physical** one, based on the workflow for your company and your team's needs.

- Have the **minimum amount of columns** possible. Anything over 7 is overkill.

- All your **tickets apply to the present workflow but also embody the complete process**.

- All your **tickets are "high level,"** meaning not every little task is accounted for, but rather represents a story.

- **Items in your backlog have direct links to tickets.**

- **Name the tickets with clear and succinct labels**.

- You have provided **clear conditions for "Definition of To-Do" and "Definition of Done"** to which your team refers ensuring they meet the expectations before moving to the next step.

- **Balance your workflow** through team-capacity WIP limits and plans for handling bottlenecks and "showstoppers." Keep lists "well fed" so team members always have something to move on to next.

- **Reject items that do not meet the standards**. Not meeting standards can refer to items of poor quality or overly large products or outputs that do not fulfill the "definition of done."

- **Assign a team member to each task in the "doing" list** otherwise the task is back to "to do."

- **You have a system in place to check the "done" items are really done.**

Structuring Your Board for Your Team

The columns on your board represent how a project reaches completion from the beginning creation phase. Each stage of this process is represented and is considered the "pipeline" of your work. A Kanban system prefers blurring the line between "stage" and "state," offering columns with the "state" of the project task, such as "doing," instead of saying something like, "analysis" or "testing."

In a lot of settings, you will know what is happening during the state of the task depending on who is working on it, so it is unnecessary to break it into more granular "stages." Some teams; however, desire and value a few more "doing" options. These additional columns represent the needs specific to the project or team. Common examples of additional "doing" columns include:

- "Ready" or "Next up to be selected."
- "Ready for Analysis" or "Ready to Define"
- "Develop" or "Implement"
- "Integrate" or other dependencies from the outside
- "Test"
- "Done" or "Complete"

Adding these additional columns between "to do" and "done" may be overkill for small companies or certain structures while more complex and large organizations will appreciate the visual progression for each stage of the process.

Notes on the Additional Columns

"Ready of Analysis" or "Ready to Define"

These distinctions are only useful for actions in a specific workflow close to other actions and directly needs to function before another action is taken. In many environments, this is an unnecessary column. Instead, the role of analysis should have its own board. This is because most analysis occurs prior to a products completion. Large amounts of analysis are piled in this column and create delays that are not relevant to the completion of the project. Instead, keep these actions independent, if possible.

"Ready"

This means you have to create a "definition of ready." This clarifies the conditions that must be met before the task is ready to work on. Then when an item is placed on the list, it is placed according to its priority level. The highest priority items are on the top and the lowest at the bottom. Each time an item is moved to this column its priority level must be considered.

"Doing"

These are columns are all about development, but sometimes, especially if you do not have a "Ready to Define" column, the actions in this column require analysis to be completed. If you opt to remove the "Ready for Analysis," include the one-off analysis requirements in this list.

"Test"

This is another optional column that can be a waste of time, depending on your industry. For example, companies that are regulated by outside agencies that will need to review your production before completion or deployment benefit from having this additional column. Other industries that do their own internal testing should consider removing this column and including the actions in the other activities. Often "testing" is done when a task is ready to move to the next location to make sure the product is "good" before passing it to someone else or to the next stage in the process.

"Done" or "Complete"

These are exactly what the terms mean: the task is finished. Your "Definition of Done" is critical at this point because it makes sure your team members only place items on this list when they meet your standards for being considered "complete." For many industries, "done" is when a product is released or is ready to be released. It does not mean it is waiting on something external to occur or the item is placed on hold. The definition will vary from business to business, but it should never provide a place to hide remaining work.

"Integrate"

If your company finds that it completes their activity on the task but it then has to wait for an external action, consider including the "Integrate" column. This is the location your team can place something when it is waiting for this outside condition. Sometimes this "integrate" can occur in the middle of development or at the end, so where the card moves to after "Integrate" depends on your workflow and product.

"Relevance"

While not a direct column, "relevance" refers to the items that the team is working on or planning to work on in the upcoming and near future or for the upcoming release. If it is part of a larger body of work, make sure the actions related to the part selected are on your board and nothing else, so it remains free from noise and volatility.

Chapter 10

The Difference Between Kanban and PAR

PAR systems are still the most common method for healthcare companies to manage medications and supplies. Hospitals are the systems that use it the most. PAR requires each item to have a level set for it. When it drops below "par", it needs to be restocked. The concept is simple; however, to determine "par," inventory conducted manually and counting in a cycle is required. The supply chain is burdened by the added manpower and cost these actions require because the activity does not add value to the system.

Unfortunately, another common practice is to guess at the inventory levels of an item, not physically count each item. This saves time; however, it is inaccurate and can cause waste. It can increase costs and inventory levels. Understanding the opportunity for error, it should come as no surprise why leading manufacturing companies do not utilize this method, despite similar goals: always have on hand a consistent amount of inventory.

The Kanban process, on the other hand, reduces non-value adding activity, like physically counting inventory, because of its visual nature. Each bin has a set number. When it is empty, it is restocked with that number. While it is waiting to be restocked, another bin is being pulled from. Because of the clear advantages of the Kanban system over the PAR methodology, many healthcare systems are beginning to change their processes to a Kanban system. Professionals involved in inventory management for hospitals and healthcare environments have reported positive results thanks to the extra time they now have to focus on valuable activities due to less time spent in the storeroom and ridding of the need for a daily inventory count.

Why Kanban Method Should Replace PAR

There are seven reasons that a Kanban process is a preferential methodology for inventory control over the PAR system.

1. The practice of properly managing inventory is promoted through a Kanban system, not through PAR. Eyeballing the bins to determine if an item is below par is not a good practice, but physically counting each item would require intense amounts of labor and is virtually impossible, especially in larger systems. Keeping the storeroom orderly and "clean" can be maintained easily with a Kanban process, while it cannot be with PAR.

2. The discipline required to restock inventory is easy to maintain with a Kanban system. A set number for each item is marked on the bin label, making it very simple for the handler to know exactly how much should be restocked for that item. It is easy and accurate each time. This means Kanban methodology can prevent shortages much better than the PAR system.

3.   Inventory is lean. Does it sound attractive to you to have 50% less inventory on hand and still meet your customer's need consistently? It should! Imagine all the cost, time, and space savings you will experience! 50% is the average inventory reduction PAR users had experienced when they switched to a Kanban practice without compromising their inventory targets.

4.   Improvement and management are easier to achieve with the Kanban process. The amount of time between depletion and restocking can be tracked. This information can then be used to set the quantity in each bin appropriately. In addition, this information can be adjusted easily if the supplier's shipping times change or demand is different. PAR makes this management and improvement hard because it restocks items every day, in undetermined quantities.

5.   Fixed quantities for replenishment are possible with Kanban processes. PAR requires the daily counting, costing your team a lot of time. Instead, their efforts can be focused elsewhere because a Kanban system provides a fixed amount needed to be ordered and visually signaled by the empty bin. It is a much simpler process.

6.   Trips to resupply are reduced with a Kanban process. Bins are refilled when it is needed, not on a daily basis, as it is with the PAR system. This means your trips to restock a bin is greatly reduced. Some Kanban practitioners have estimated their trips to restock have been cut down by as much as 50%.

7.   Since bins are not refilled every day, counting does not need to happen every day, as it is required with the PAR system. Kanban methods keep the process as simple as possible: when the bin is empty, reorder the fixed number for

that item. While you wait for it to be restocked you pull from the second bin for the product. You continue to pull from that second bin even if the first bin stock arrives before it is empty.

When the second bin is empty, you move the first bin forward and pull from it while the second bin is being restocked. The cycle continues on a loop, refining and improving over time. Not spending all that time counting while using the PAR system will save your company hundreds, maybe even thousands, of man-hours each year! Imagine the improved efficiency and cost-savings.

Inventory management for all healthcare and hospital systems should use a Kanban system over a PAR system. In fact, any industry that must regulate inventory should consider utilizing a Kanban system over the "eyeball the stock" approach of PAR. The industry and your organization can expect enormous financial savings thanks to the reduction in inventory, a minimal shortage, and improved productivity.

How to Easily Change from a PAR to a Kanban System

Because of the obvious advantages of a Kanban process over a PAR system, you may be wondering how it is best to change processes and also avoid errors and frustration. As with anything new, it is best to roll it out in a simple and clear manner after you get the buy-in from all the people involved, including your suppliers! Thankfully, there are technological solutions out there that you can consider to help make the transition easier for your company.

Spacesaver

On the shelf, in front of the two bins containing materials, there is an RFID tag. When an inventory manager recognizes the front bin is empty, they scan the RFID tag and move the empty bin behind the second, full bin. When the tag is scanned, it alerts the person or department in charge of ordering what needs to be refilled. The reason RFID tags were chosen is that they tend to be more accurate and uses less time than a barcode that is printed on a Kanban card or on the box. Of course, RFID tags and the reader cost extra money.

PAR Excellence

To minimize the manpower required even further, PAR Excellence looks to remove not just counting but also scanning barcodes or RFID tags. Instead of tags, scales are placed under the bins. A weight is associated with a full and empty bin. When the bin reaches the empty weight, it signals the person or department in charge of ordering the need to restock that particular item. As with the other solution presented above, this system adds the initial cost of installing scales in your stockroom, and each scale needs to be calibrated for the inventory item and set up on a specific network. Then you need to monitor and maintain a lot of associated data

Logi-D

Similar to Spacesaver, this solution offers an RFID tag to reorder the item that is depleted. Instead of scanning the tag and returning the tag to the shelf, like Spacesaver, Logi-D has a board located on a stockroom wall, which collects the tags of all the items that are being restocked. When the tag is removed from the shelf the empty tag space is colored red, signaling quickly to your inventory manager that the tag is on the wall for reorder.

Technology is "cool" and exciting, but it is an added cost to consider. Do not jump on any technology "bandwagon" because it is new and looks fancy. Choose a system if you think you need it because you see the value it can add to your organization. If it helps, choose a solution. If it does not, keep it simple with a card or a bin.

Conclusion

Thanks for making it through to the end of *Kanban: The Complete Step-by-Step Guide to Agile Project Management with Kanban.* Let's hope it was informative and able to provide you with all the tools you need to achieve your goals.

Your next step is to observe and plan your transformation. Stop wondering how you can become more lean, agile, and efficient. You just read all about it! Now is the time for action. Now is the time to prepare your Kanban board and visual system to make your life easier and your team happier. Now is the time to lower costs and increase production using a simple and effective method.

While you are planning, get the buy-in from your team, company, stakeholders, and even your customers. Sell them on the benefits of adopting a Kanban system, and stay close to the process, refining as needed, so it is the most efficient system for your business. Remember, the goal of this is to assist your team members in working alongside one another efficiently while also benefiting your company. Keeping your eye on this goal during each decision you make will help with all the changes and challenges.

A Kanban methodology applies to a variety of situations, despite rumors it is "outdated." As it is with new technology, do not jump onto the glossy "bandwagon." You have read the options and reviews. Determine the unique needs of your organization and create a way to make this basic system work for you. Do not forget, before you roll out your Kanban board;

compare them against the checklist in Chapter 9 to make sure they are "good!" It is a great practice to do each and every time, or at least until you have a firm grasp on the process. The more and more you use boards, lists, and cards, the better your team will get at running an effective Kanban project and process. As they continue to feel empowered and successful, imagine the positive atmosphere and engaged work environment you will have! Success will come to you in a variety of forms thanks to you implementing this methodology in your company. Congratulations on taking this step towards a more productive future for your company!

Finally, if you found this book useful in any way, a review on Amazon is always appreciated!

Made in the USA
Coppell, TX
01 March 2022

74296758R00042